Fact Finders®

THE LINCOLN *Memorial*

MYTHS, Legends, and FACTS

by Katie Clark

Consultant:
Melodie Andrews, PhD
Associate Professor of History
Minnesota State University
Mankato, Minnesota

CAPSTONE PRESS

Fact Finders Books are published by Capstone Press,
1710 Roe Crest Drive, North Mankato, Minnesota 56003
www.capstonepub.com

Library of Congress Cataloging-in-Publication Data
Cataloging-in-publication information is on file with the Library of Congress.
ISBN 978-1-4914-0205-4 (library binding)
ISBN 978-1-4914-0210-8 (pbk.)
ISBN 978-1-4914-0214-6 (ebook pdf)

Editorial Credits
Bobbie Nuytten, lead designer; Charmaine Whitman, production specialist

Developed and Produced by Focus Strategic Communications, Inc.
Adrianna Edwards: project manager
Ron Edwards, Kelly Stern: editors
Rob Scanlan: designer and compositor
Karen Hunter: media researcher
Francine Geraci: copy editor and proofreader
Wendy Scavuzzo: fact checker

Photo Credits
Alamy: David Coleman, 17; Deborah Crowle Illustrations, 13 (top); Dreamstime: Glenn Nagel, 26; Historical Society
of the Lower Cape Fear, 12; iStockphoto: ajansen, 16 (top), ninjaMonkeyStudio, 21; Landov: DPA, 25; Library of
Congress, 4, 6, 9, 11, 15, 16 (bottom), 20, 24; National Archives and Records Administration, 10, 18; North Wind
Picture Archives, 7; Shutterstock: Africa Studio, 23, Anthony Correia, 27, Brandon Bourdages, cover (right), 1 (right),
back cover, Claudio Divizia (stamp), cover, 1, Drimi, 14, ES James, 19, Givaga, 22 (bottom left and right), Jorge
Salcedo, 5, Konstantin L, 8, Michael Shake, 22 (middle), Orhan Cam, cover (bottom), 1 (bottom), 3, 28–29, Robynrg
(dollar bill), cover, 1, Sascha Burkard, 13 (bottom); Wikipedia: Edward Stabler (presidential seal), cover, 1

Design Elements by Shutterstock

Printed in the United States of America in Stevens Point, Wisconsin.
032014   008092WZF14

Table of Contents

HONORING LINCOLN

The nation's capital, Washington, D.C., is home to the president and other government leaders. But its many **monuments** make the city truly unique. Monuments honor past presidents, famous scientists, and the men and women who fought in wars. All of these monuments have something in common. They help us remember how certain people and events helped shape the nation.

A grand columned monument overlooks the city's National Mall. Inside the monument is a large marble sculpture of Abraham Lincoln. The monument is both beautiful and mysterious. What do its columns mean? Who built the structure? What words surround Lincoln? Answers to these questions can be found within the monument itself.

monument: a statue or building that is meant to remind people of an event or a person

the Lincoln Memorial overlooking the National Mall

The Lincoln Memorial is the center of many rumors, legends, and myths.

Who Was Lincoln?

As the nation's 16th president, Lincoln is known for keeping the country united during a time of civil war. Lincoln took office in March 1861. Soon after, the Civil War erupted. Southern states were angered by Lincoln's election and feared he would end slavery. Black people were taken from Africa by force and sold as slaves. Southern states relied on slaves to work their plantations. These states soon **seceded** from the Union and formed the **Confederate** States of America. The Civil War soon followed.

Lincoln believed the war was about keeping the nation together and settling the issue of slavery. He issued the Emancipation Proclamation and pushed Congress to pass the 13th Amendment, officially ending slavery across the country.

secede: to withdraw formally from a group or an organization, often to form another organization

Confederate: a person who supported the South during the Civil War

Lincoln's nickname was "Honest Abe." Many people trusted what he said and believed he would be fair.

Shortly after the end of the Civil War, Lincoln was **assassinated**. Across the country people were shocked and devastated by the loss of their president.

Despite Lincoln's death more than 150 years ago, he is considered by many to be the greatest U.S. president. Lincoln's leadership during the Civil War is viewed as a defining moment in the nation's history. His historic speeches, including the Gettysburg Address, are still recited and studied today by leaders around the world.

assassinate: to murder a person who is well known or important

Abraham Lincoln delivered the Gettysburg Address on November 19, 1863.

LINCOLN, THE MEMORIAL

Shortly after Lincoln's death, leaders discussed making a **memorial** for the fallen president. They wanted to build a monument. Several memorial sculptures were done of Lincoln following his death, including a full-length marble statue of Lincoln unveiled in 1868.

As these commemorative efforts continued, Congress worked to create a larger national memorial for Lincoln. The Lincoln Monument Association worked with a sculptor to create plans for a 36-figure bronze monument. But this idea was never completed.

The Lincoln Monument Association asked for donations to pay for the project. They worked on it for many years, but they ran into problems. Soon the money they had raised was gone. Over time they gave up, and the idea of a memorial was set aside.

one of the first statues of Lincoln, 1868

memorial: something that is built or done to help people remember a person or event

The Lincoln Memorial Commission

But not everyone gave up. Illinois Senator Shelby Cullom had been a friend of Lincoln's. He pushed for a formal memorial site. The Senate Park Commission devised plans for a Lincoln Memorial as part of an expanded National Mall. It took 10 years and six tries before Congress finally approved the site on the bank of the Potomac River for the memorial.

In 1910, years after Lincoln's death, a group was formed to make the new memorial. It was called the Lincoln Memorial Commission. This commission would honor the 16th president with a national memorial.

members of the Lincoln Memorial Commission

Planning the Memorial

The Lincoln Memorial Commission searched for an **architect** to design the monument. The members wanted a memorial that would capture Lincoln's legacy and the American spirit. Henry Bacon and John Pope were the two men who competed for the job. They drew plans for the monument to show to the commission.

The members of the commission liked both men's ideas. They chose Bacon's designs. His plans were grand and still fit the budget.

architect: a person who designs and draws plans for buildings, bridges, and other construction projects

John Pope's design for the Lincoln Memorial was not chosen. Later he designed the Jefferson Memorial and the National Gallery of Art.

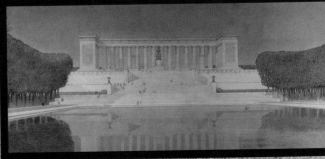

Henry Bacon's design for the Lincoln Memorial was inspired by classic Greek temples.

SUGGESTIONS FOR THE LINCOLN MEMORIAL

For a long time, no one could agree on what Lincoln's memorial should be. A statue seemed like a good idea. Other ideas were a memorial road from Washington, D.C., to Gettysburg, Pennsylvania, or a bridge across the Potomac River. Another suggestion was a log cabin like the one where Lincoln grew up.

Lincoln's log cabin

Choosing the Site

By now it was 1911. Before work on the monument could begin, the commission needed to select a site. The commission chose a spot near the Potomac River. It was next to the Washington Monument and the Capitol Building and would expand the National Mall. But it was also set apart from these structures. This would let people be "alone" with Lincoln.

Lincoln's followers put up a fight. The land near the river was a swamp. They said Lincoln deserved a better spot. But the commission's choice and Bacon's winning design won out. The Lincoln Memorial would be built at last.

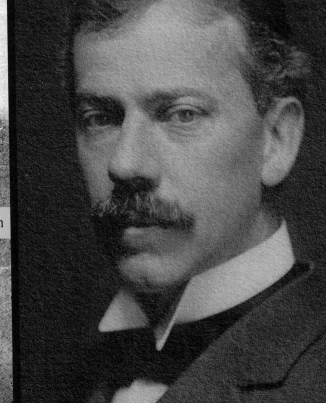

Henry Bacon

Map of the National Mall

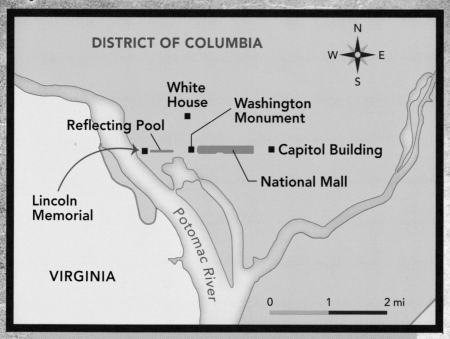

The Lincoln Memorial is at the west end of the National Mall. It faces the Washington Monument and the Capitol Building.

AMERICAN PENNY

The year 1909 was the 100th anniversary of Lincoln's birth. The U.S. Mint decided to come out with a one-cent coin with Lincoln's image on it. Victor David Brenner designed the coin using the profile of Lincoln's head. The U.S. penny has had the same image ever since. The reverse side of the penny had several designs over the years. But one of the most famous is the Lincoln Memorial. Today the union shield appears on the reverse side.

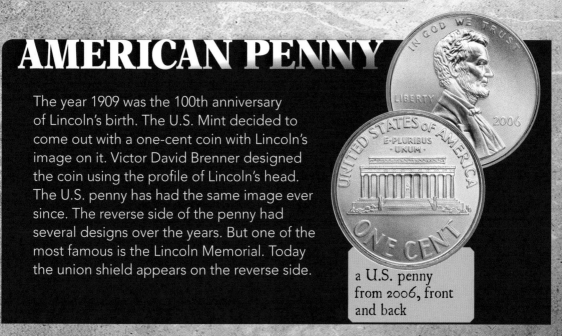

a U.S. penny from 2006, front and back

THE BUILDING

Rumors about Bacon's design started right away. Some people said the building held hidden messages. They wanted to know what Bacon was trying to say. But Bacon had no secrets. He had thought a lot about his design for the Lincoln Memorial. He wanted something that showed what Lincoln believed in.

Lincoln believed in a "government of the people, by the people, for the people." This **democratic** form of government began in ancient Greece where certain citizens had the right to vote.

Bacon decided to have the monument look like a Greek temple called the Parthenon. Both buildings have large columns on the outside and open space on the inside. The Parthenon is considered the birthplace of democracy.

democratic: having a kind of government in which citizens vote for their leaders

Construction Begins

The memorial's construction began in 1914 with work on the outer building. Drainage pipes and concrete piers were used to secure the swampy land. They provided a strong foundation.

Most of the work on the outer building was finished by 1917 when the United States entered World War I (1914–1918). Work on the inside of the building moved along at a much slower pace. With so many skilled workers fighting the war in Europe, work on the project slowed.

Bacon made sure that construction material used in the building came from all over the country. He saw the completion of the columns, festoons, steps and hall, and finally the statue of Lincoln, which is the centerpiece of the monument.

the Lincoln Memorial under construction

FACT Bacon insisted on using building materials from different states. That way all states would be part of the memorial. The marble ceiling tiles were from Alabama. Lincoln's statue was made from Georgia granite. Marble from Colorado was brought in for the columns.

The Columns

Bacon wanted the memorial to stand for the things that make the United States a strong nation. He started with the states. The country had 36 states when Lincoln was alive. Bacon wanted to honor those states that Lincoln had worked so hard to keep together as a unified nation. He designed 36 huge columns to surround the building.

columns of the Lincoln Memorial

The Festoons

At the top of the 36 columns are amazing carvings called festoons. The country had 48 states when the memorial was built. So Bacon included 48 festoons in his design. New festoons were added to the memorial when Alaska and Hawaii became states.

Ernest C. Bairstow was hired to sculpt the festoons on the Lincoln Memorial.

Mysterious Steps

The famous marble steps leading to the monument have been a source of myths since construction began on the monument. Some people believed the number of steps held a secret message. There are 57 steps. People said that Bacon had built a step for every year of Lincoln's life, but Lincoln died at age 56.

The Halls and Speeches

Bacon's design included a hall on each side of Lincoln's statue. The halls hold two of Lincoln's most famous speeches. On the south wall is the Gettysburg Address. It was chosen because it was familiar to many people, and it showed Lincoln's determination to keep the country united. The other speech on the north wall is his Second Inaugural Address, which represented reunion.

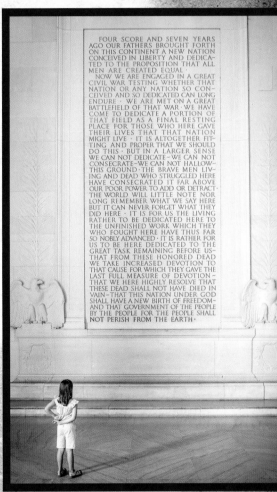

FACT The carvers of the Second Inaugural Address accidently carved an E instead of an F. The bottom line of the E was quickly filled in with putty, changing it to an F. Visitors can still see the mistake.

the carving of the Gettysburg Address in the Lincoln Memorial

THE STATUE

Daniel Chester French was chosen to **sculpt** the statue of Lincoln. French had done many other great statues, such as "The Minute Man." It was sculpted to honor men who fought in the American Revolutionary War.

French began work on the statue at the same time the builders started on the outer memorial. He first designed a bronze statue of Lincoln to be 10 feet (3 meters) tall. But the 60-foot (18.3 m) memorial halls dwarfed the statue. French also saw that much of the building was marble. He knew a marble statue would look better than a bronze one. He went back to work and changed his plans. It took four years, but the statue of Lincoln ended up being 19 feet (5.8 m) tall. It was made of 28 blocks of marble from Georgia. It was so large that it had to be brought inside in pieces.

sculpt: to create art by carving stone, wood, or other materials

The Lincoln Memorial statue shows Lincoln seated on a huge chair.

Relative Heights

Relative Heights	Feet and Inches	Metric
adult	5 feet, 5 inches	165 cm
school bus	9 feet	2.7 m
one-story house	16 feet	4.9 m
Lincoln Memorial statue	19 feet	5.8 m
Lincoln Memorial building	99 feet	30.2 m

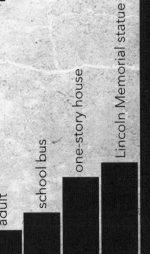

Myth of Lincoln's Hair

Just as there were myths about the building, there were myths about Lincoln's statue too. Some still exist today.

Many people find their eyes drawn to the president's hair. Some say the tufts of hair on the back of his head look like the face of Robert E. Lee. Lee was the commander of the Confederate Army during the Civil War. Others think they see Jefferson Davis, president of the Confederacy. Still others see Ulysses S. Grant, commander of the Union Army, in Lincoln's carved hair.

Robert E. Lee

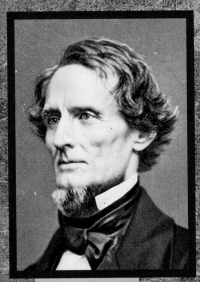
Jefferson Davis

Ulysses S. Grant

People wonder if French did this on purpose. But French denied this claim. In sculpting Lincoln, French studied photographs of the late president's hair. Lincoln was known for his coarse hair that often looked unbrushed. When carved into marble, Lincoln's unruly locks took on a life of their own. French was simply trying to create a detailed sculpture of Lincoln from head to toe.

profile of Lincoln's statue

Lincoln's Hands

Over the years a legend has grown about the hands on Lincoln's statue. One hand is relaxed. The other is closed. People noticed that the relaxed right hand looks like the letter "L" in American Sign Language. The closed left hand looks like the letter "A."

Daniel French's son was deaf. Because of this, French was familiar with sign language. People believe French sculpted Lincoln's hands to resemble his initials, "A. L."

But this is a myth. French said the closed fist stood for Lincoln's determination. The open hand stood for his compassion. If the hands looked like anything else, French said, it was only by chance.

Many people believe Lincoln's hands may be indicating sign language.

SIGN LANGUAGE

Sign language is used to communicate without speaking. This system is generally used by people who cannot hear well or who cannot speak. There are hundreds of different sign language systems used around the world. American Sign Language is used in the United States and Canada.

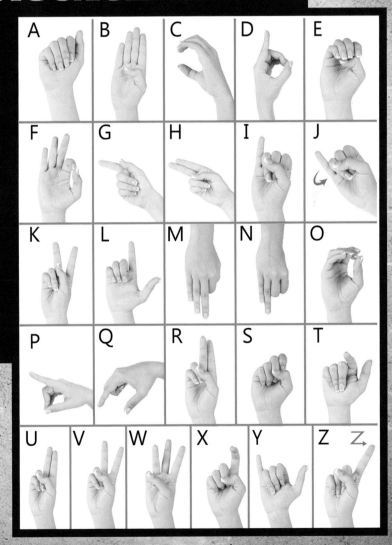

23

THE MEMORIAL TODAY

It took eight years to build the Lincoln Memorial. It was finally finished in 1922. At last, the people could visit a national memorial in honor of a great leader.

A grand celebration was held on the opening day. Many important guests were invited. President Warren G. Harding came. So did Lincoln's son, Robert T. Lincoln. Former President and Chief Justice William Howard Taft gave the **dedication** speech.

dedication: a ceremony marking the official completion or opening of a building or monument

The Memorial Commission had planned for only 5,000 people at the opening ceremony. But almost 50,000 arrived. They did not have enough food or seats.

The Memorial and Equal Rights

The Lincoln Memorial has long stood for equal rights. In 1939 African-American singer Marian Anderson was not allowed to perform in Constitution Hall in Washington, D.C., because of her race. First lady Eleanor Roosevelt secured the Lincoln Memorial steps. There Anderson sang for the world to hear.

The Lincoln Memorial was also the site of a major event in the civil rights movement. In 1963 Dr. Martin Luther King Jr. gave his famous "I Have a Dream" speech from its steps. The National Mall was packed with people listening to King's words on equality.

Martin Luther King Jr. after speaking at the Lincoln Memorial

What Lies Beneath?

When people think of memorials, they often think of graveyards and tombstones. Many people believe that Lincoln's body is buried under his memorial.

But this is a myth. After his death Lincoln's body was taken to Springfield, Illinois. There he was buried at the Oak Ridge Cemetery.

Lots of people want to know what is under the memorial. There is a huge dark basement with concrete and steel support columns under the building. There are also tunnels that helped the builders move from one side to the other.

Lincoln's tomb in Springfield, Illinois

Lincoln's Ghost?

Tour guides used to take visitors through the old tunnels. Former guides tell stories of flashing lights and slamming doors. They believed ghosts haunted the tunnels. Some claimed Lincoln's ghost wandered down there. Others thought it was the ghosts of workers who helped build the memorial. The tunnels are no longer open to the public.

VANDALISM

In July 2013 the Lincoln Memorial was closed. Someone splashed green paint on the statue. The paint was carefully cleaned off. The memorial was opened again later the same day. There was no permanent damage.

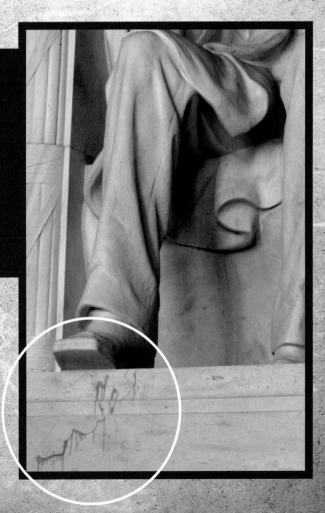

Remembering a Hero

Today the Lincoln Memorial is almost 100 years old. It is a symbol of unity and equal rights. It stands for democracy in America.

Since its early design and construction, the Lincoln Memorial has been a source of myth and mystery. More than 6 million people visit the monument each year to honor the man and check out the many myths for themselves. This grand marble structure stands as the ultimate honor to one of the nation's greatest leaders.

the Lincoln Memorial lit up at night

GLOSSARY

architect (AR-ki-tekt)—a person who designs and draws plans for buildings, bridges, and other construction projects

assassinate (us-SASS-uh-nate)—to murder a person who is well known or important

Confederate (kuhn-FE-der-uht)—a person who supported the South during the Civil War

dedication (ded-uh-KAY-shuhn)—a ceremony marking the official completion or opening of a building or monument

democratic (de-muh-KRA-tik)—having a kind of government in which citizens vote for their leaders

memorial (muh-MOR-ee-uhl)—something that is built or done to help people remember a person or event

monument (MON-yuh-muhnt)—a statue or building that is meant to remind people of an event or a person

sculpt (SKUHLPT)—to create art by carving stone, wood, or other materials

secede (si-SEED)—to withdraw formally from a group or an organization, often to form another organization

READ MORE

Erin, Audrey. *Visit the Lincoln Memorial*. Landmarks of Liberty. New York: Gareth Stevens Pub. 2012.

Marcovitz, Hal. *Lincoln Memorial: Shrine to an American Hero*. Patriotic Symbols of America. Broomall, Pa.: Mason Crest, 2014.

Nelson, Kristin L. *The Lincoln Memorial*. Famous Places. Minneapolis: Lerner Publication Co., 2011.

CRITICAL THINKING USING THE COMMON CORE

1. Reread the text on page 25. Why is it special that Marian Anderson and Martin Luther King Jr. were heard on the steps of the Lincoln Memorial? How do you think Abraham Lincoln would have felt if he had heard them? Why? Which details in the text support your answer? You may also add more evidence using your background knowledge of the president. (Key Ideas and Details)

2. Reread pages 28-29. What is the author's point of view? Is the author relating information, or is she trying to convince you to agree with her point of view, or both? Explain your answer using evidence from the section. Now find a section in the book that just shares information. What makes the two sections different? (Craft and Structure)

3. Examine these images: the photo of the Gettysburg Address on page 17, the photo of the statue under construction on page 18, and the photo of the opening of the memorial on page 24. Next, examine the bar graph on page 19. How do these images help you understand the size of the memorial and the statue? Which one helped you the most? Why? (Integration of Knowledge and Ideas)

INTERNET SITES

FactHound offers a safe, fun way to find Internet sites related to this book. All of the sites on FactHound have been researched by our staff.

Here's all you do:

Visit *www.facthound.com*

Type in this code: 9781491402054

Check out projects, games, and lots more at
www.capstonekids.com

Super-cool stuff!

INDEX

18(1)

19 99